GIFTED
&
TALENTED®

To develop
your child's gifts
and talents

READING COMPREHENSION
BOOK TWO

A Workbook for Ages 6–8

Written by S. J. Williams, M.A.
Illustrated by Larry Nolte

LOWELL HOUSE JUVENILE

LOS ANGELES

NTC/Contemporary Publishing Group

In gratitude to the Chilkat.
—S.J.W.

Published by Lowell House
A division of NTC/Contemporary Publishing Group, Inc.
4255 West Touhy Avenue, Lincolnwood (Chicago), Illinois 60646-1975 U.S.A.

Managing Director and Publisher: Jack Artenstein
Director of Publishing Services: Rena Copperman
Editorial Director, Juvenile: Brenda Pope-Ostrow
Director of Art Production: Bret Perry
Educational Editor: Linda Gorman
Designer: Victor W. Perry

Lowell House books can be purchased at special discounts when ordered in bulk for premiums and special sales. Please contact Customer Service at:
NTC/Contemporary Publishing Group
4255 W. Touhy Avenue
Lincolnwood, IL 60646-1975
1-800-323-4900

Printed and bound in the United States of America

ISBN: 0-7373-0050-7

10 9 8 7 6 5 4 3 2

GIFTED & TALENTED® WORKBOOKS will help develop your child's natural talents and gifts by providing activities to enhance critical and creative thinking skills. These skills of logic and reasoning teach children **how to think**. They are precisely the skills emphasized by teachers of gifted and talented children.

Thinking skills are the skills needed to be able to learn anything at any time. Unlike events, words, and teaching methods, thinking skills never change. If a child has a grasp of how to think, school success and even success in life will become more assured. In addition, the child will become self-confident as he or she approaches new tasks with the ability to think them through and discover solutions.

GIFTED & TALENTED® WORKBOOKS present these skills in a unique way, combining the basic subject areas of reading, language arts, and math with thinking skills. The top of each page is labeled to indicate the specific thinking skill developed. Here are some of the skills you will find:

- Deduction—the ability to reach a logical conclusion by interpreting clues

- Understanding Relationships—the ability to recognize how objects, shapes, and words are similar or dissimilar; to classify or categorize

- Sequencing—the ability to organize events, numbers; to recognize patterns

- Inference—the ability to reach a logical conclusion from given or assumed evidence

- Creative Thinking—the ability to generate unique ideas; to compare and contrast the same elements in different situations; to present imaginative solutions to problems

GIFTED & TALENTED® WORKBOOKS have been written and endorsed by educators. These books will benefit any child who demonstrates curiosity, imagination, a sense of fun and wonder about the world, and a desire to learn. They will open your child's mind to new experiences and help fulfill his or her true potential.

This *Reading Comprehension Workbook* is designed to give children the opportunity to develop their ability to understand, as well as build upon, what they read. Reading comprehension—the process of extracting meaning from written material—involves a complex set of skills. In order to understand what he or she has read, a young reader must be able to:

- Use picture and contextual clues to develop word meaning
- Identify the main idea in a written passage
- Recognize word clues and understand their importance
- Order the sequence of events in a written passage
- Locate details and relate them to the main idea
- Predict reasonable outcomes
- Draw conclusions based on inference

Notice that on some pages, there is more than one answer. Accept your child's response and then challenge him or her to come up with another. Also, where the child is asked to write, remember that the expression of his or her ideas is more important than spelling. At this age, the child should be encouraged to record the letter sounds he or she hears without fear of mistakes. This process is known as invented spelling. Using invented spelling permits your child's spoken vocabulary to be available to him or her for writing.

So, if your child writes *dnosr* for *dinosaur*, that's okay! Praise your child for the sounds he or she hears and the answer he or she comes up with. Then help your child to fill in the missing vowels to spell the word correctly.

The activities should be done consecutively, as they become increasingly challenging from page to page. You may need to work with your child on many of the pages. If necessary, help your child read and understand the directions before going on. Use your child's interest as a gauge. If he or she becomes tired or frustrated, stop working. A page or two at a time may be enough, as the child should have fun while learning.

Read each group of words. Circle the one word in each group that tells about the other words in that group.

rock and roll
jazz
hip hop
music
classical

soft
pillow
feathers
cotton
snow

glue
sticky
gum
tape
syrup

wrench
saw
hammer
pliers
tool

Now make up a story using at least one word from each group.

Read each group of words. Circle the one word in each group that tells about the other words in that group.

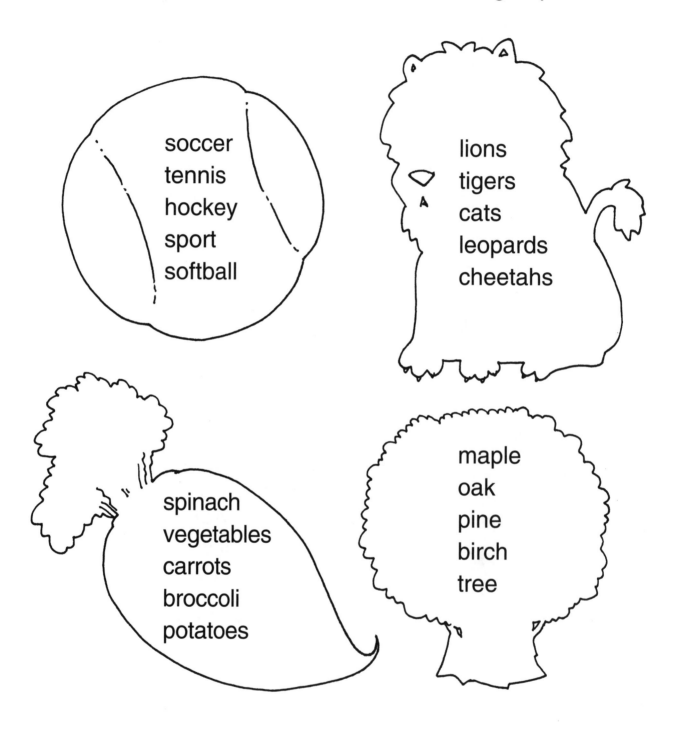

soccer
tennis
hockey
sport
softball

lions
tigers
cats
leopards
cheetahs

spinach
vegetables
carrots
broccoli
potatoes

maple
oak
pine
birch
tree

Now make up a story using at least one word from each group.

Read the statements about the picture below. Then color the picture to make every statement true.

The animal toy inside the toy chest is brown.
The round toy is purple.
The toy next to the round toy is red.
The toy that can fly is orange.
The objects you wear on your feet are the color you get when you mix yellow and blue.

Make each sentence below a true statement by adding something to the picture on the next page. Use crayons to add color where necessary. One of the statements is already true. Using the picture to help you, find that statement and circle it.

Three children are seated at their desks.

A boy is watering the plants.

A girl is drawing a picture of her cat.

The teacher's desk has four drawers.

The teacher is writing "Reading Time" on the blackboard.

The children at their desks are holding red books.

There is a gray mouse under the teacher's desk.

There is a green apple on the teacher's desk.

The flag is red, white, and blue.

Draw a line to connect each string of words on the left with a string of words on the right to make a complete sentence. Make sure that each sentence you form makes sense.

Hint: There are several ways to connect the groups of words. Try out different combinations to find the ones you like best.

The old woman	stayed up late marking tests.
The gray kitten	wore yellow sneakers.
The tired teacher	used a cane to walk.
The oak tree	painted a colorful picture.
The little girl	made a delicious meal.
The talented artist	lost its leaves in the winter.
The great chef	curled up on the blanket.

Draw a line from each group of words on the left to the word on the right that could go after each word in the group.

blue humming song	cake
cup sponge layer	cheese
sweet green black-eyed	chip
Swiss cheddar jack	bird
potato corn chocolate	pea

Make up a title for each picture and write it on the line. Your title should tell what the picture is about in just a few words.

Title: _____

Title: _____

Make up a title for each picture and write it on the line. Your title should tell what the picture is about in just a few words.

Title:_____

Title:_____

Read the story below. Then color the picture that fits the story.

Elmo the elephant went for a walk in the forest one day. He was enjoying the sounds of the birds and the warmth of the sun on his back. Suddenly, he felt a sharp pain in his foot. He had stepped on a thorn! Elmo heard a small voice coming from under a nearby bush. "I can help you," it said. The voice belonged to a mouse, whose tiny paws were just the right size to take out the thorn in Elmo's foot.

Jean is looking for her sister Allison onstage. Help Jean find Allison by reading the clues below. Draw a circle around Allison.

Allison is wearing a tutu.

Allison has her hair in a bun.

Allison is wearing a heart necklace.

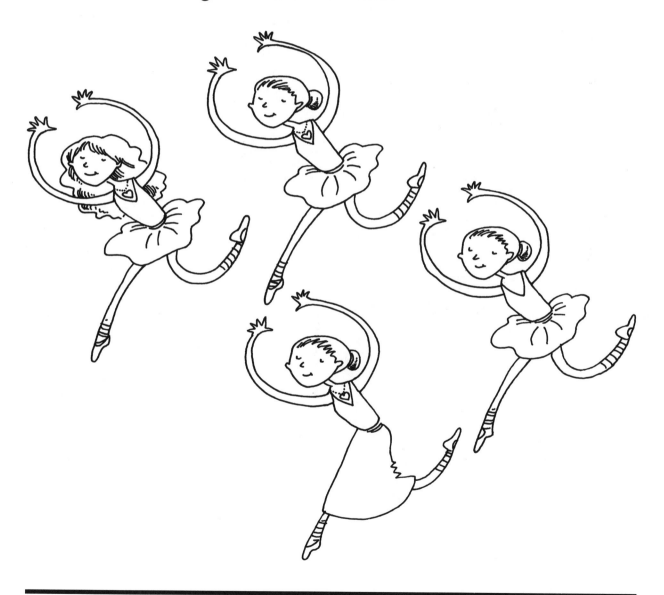

Andre wants to go traveling. He likes places that are cold. He likes to ski. He likes to visit places where the people speak a language other than English.

Circle the travel brochure that describes the place where Andre should go.

Each pair of sentences tells about the picture next to it. The first sentence in each pair makes sense. The second sentence contains a mistake. Find the mistake in the second sentence and circle it. Beneath the mistake, write a word that would make more sense in the sentence.

Robbie watched the rain.
The rain made him feel happy.

_____

It is lunchtime.
Lorna made herself a big
pumpkin to eat.

_____

Theo is an artist.
He grows pictures.

_____

Delilah is learning karate.
She can break a board
with her nose.

_____

Each pair of sentences tells about the picture next to it. The first sentence in each pair makes sense. The second sentence contains a mistake. Find the mistake in the second sentence and circle it. Beneath the mistake, write a word that would make more sense in the sentence.

Hedda's favorite snack is french fries.
She likes to eat them with sand.

_____

The elves are laughing and smiling.
They are very angry.

_____

Tommy has short hair.
He has freckles on his teeth.

_____

Salvador set the table for dinner.
He was very lazy with his
mother's fine china.

_____

For an extra challenge, use each mistake in a new sentence that makes sense.

Each pair of sentences tells about the picture next to it. The first sentence in each pair makes sense. The second sentence contains a mistake. Find the mistake in the second sentence and circle it. Beneath the mistake, write a word that would make more sense in the sentence.

The children played outside all day.
They played until the moon
went down.

_____

The horse is hungry.
It loves to eat broccoli.

_____

Bart is making a fruit salad.
He is cutting up lots of cookies.

_____

Toto's ear perked up.
He smelled a faint sound.

_____

For an extra challenge, use each mistake in a new sentence that makes sense.

Read each sentence below. Cross out the word that doesn't belong. On the blank line, write a new word that will make the sentence make sense.

Jenny put the dirty dishes in the freezer.

_____

Sissy was excited when she got lost in the store. _____

Bill sat down and grabbed the remote control to turn on the dryer. _____

Miranda pricked her ankle on a thorn when she was picking roses. _____

Jacob put on his pajamas and went to work. _____

The police officer gave the motorcycle driver a ticket for driving too quietly. _____

Read each sentence below. Cross out the word that doesn't belong. On the blank line, write a new word that will make the sentence make sense.

Mickey likes mustard and relish on his pie.

_____

"Trevor, wait for the WALK sign before you paint the street." _____

The cook placed the turkey in the dryer. _____

Aunt Edna snapped a statue of her niece. _____

The curious turtle sniffed every tree in the park during its walk.

_____

Katrina's mom needed plenty of patience to swim her daughter's curly hair. _____

Read the story. Draw a picture in the box below that shows what the story is about.

Penelope kept her pet rabbit Mopsy in a cage in the backyard. One day, Penelope went outside to feed Mopsy, but the cage door was open and Mopsy was gone! Penelope saw rabbit tracks in the dirt and followed them. The tracks led her to her neighbor's garden. Penelope looked through the green plants. She spotted a white fluffy tail. She looked closer. It was Mopsy, munching on a large orange carrot from the garden.

Below are the steps you need to follow to wash a dog, but they are all mixed up. Number the steps in order. Mark an **X** in front of any steps that are not needed.

_____ Rinse off the dog's fur.

_____ Work the shampoo into a lather.

_____ Wet the dog's fur.

_____ Catch the dog.

_____ Pour some shampoo on the dog.

_____ Dry the dog with a towel.

_____ Make sure it is a sunny day.

Read each pair of statements, then write a conclusion based on what you have read. The first one is done for you.

All elephants have trunks.
Jumbo is an elephant.
Conclusion: <u>Jumbo has a trunk.</u>

All seagulls can fly.
Jonathan is a seagull.
Conclusion: _____.

All tigers have stripes.
Samson is a tiger.
Conclusion: _____.

All pine trees have pine needles.
A ponderosa is a pine tree.
Conclusion: _____.

For an extra challenge: On a separate sheet of paper, make up your own pairs of statements. Challenge a friend or a family member to read your statements and draw conclusions.

Read the story. Fill in each blank with a word from the box below. Make sure the story makes sense.

Holly and her family went to the Grand Canyon for a vacation. They rode through the canyon on _____. They saw _____ against the backdrop of orange and red canyon walls. Holly could _____ all the trees they saw. They came upon a _____. Holly's parents were _____ until Holly told them that it was _____.

harmless	hawks	paint	name
burros	frightened	parrots	snake
camels	penguin	tired	poisonous

Lilith likes to read books about lots of different things. She likes to read about other countries. She loves stories about wild animals. She is very interested in space travel. She enjoys baking.

Look at the books below. Circle only the books that Lilith would like to read.

José's music teacher is teaching his class a new song. The song is about a genie who comes out of a special lamp and makes wishes come true.

Which words below do you think might be in the song? Circle them.

magic	hopes
ocean	wand
rub	granted
wish	surprise
money	homework
happiness	candy
smoke	disappear

If you had three wishes, what would they be?

1. _____

2. _____

3. _____

Read each sentence below. Then read each statement that follows. Using the information in the first sentence, decide which word best completes each statement. Then write that word on the line.

Harvey put on his rain jacket before going fishing.

Harvey wanted to stay _____.   wet   dry

Harvey went fishing _____ he put on his rain jacket.   before   after

Harvey might catch a _____.   trout   lizard

The cottonwood trees along the highway glowed yellow and red in the fall sunshine.

_____ is ending.   Summer   Winter

The weather is _____.   cloudy   sunny

A cottonwood is a kind of _____.   plant   animal

28

Read the story. Then circle the correct answer to each question.

Sandra and Sue spent a rainy day inside the house. First, they made pancakes for breakfast. Then they cleaned their room. After that, they played hide-and-seek. Then they had tomato soup for lunch. After lunch, their mom read them a book about spiders. Then the sun came out, so they went outside and looked for spiders.

Did Sandra and Sue clean their room before or after lunch?

before   after

Did Sandra and Sue look for spiders before or after their mom read them a book?

before   after

Did Sandra and Sue eat soup before or after they played hide-and-seek?

before   after

Did Sandra and Sue eat breakfast before or after they cleaned their room?

before   after

Each sentence below contains a blank line. Beneath each sentence is a pair of words that mean the opposite of each other. Fill in the blank with the word that makes sense.

Jeremiah shivered when he stepped out into the _____ air.

warm   cold

Ramona is an honest girl who _____ lies.

never   always

Bethany used her sewing machine to _____ her clothes.

rip   mend

Steve decided to look for his lost watch during the _____ when he could see better.

day   night

Tim was _____ to be the ring bearer in his uncle's wedding.

proud   ashamed

Read each main sentence below. Then read the statements that follow. Decide if each statement is true or false and circle your answer.

The dolphins leaped and played in the lagoon. They enjoyed the sunny day.

The dolphins played in the rain.
    true   false

The dolphins were sad.
    true   false

The dolphins liked the sun.
    true   false

The tennis player won the match. She won by one point.

It was a close game.
    true   false

It was a bowling match.
    true   false

The tennis player left in a good mood.
    true   false

Read each main sentence below. Then read the statements that follow. Decide if each statement is true or false and circle your answer.

Recycling saves land and trees, and decreases the amount of trash we produce.

The more we recycle, the more trash we have.
    true   false

Recycling saves land.
    true   false

More trees are cut down because of recycling.
    true   false

Princess Elizabeth of Utopia promised her people that they would always be happy.

Elizabeth lived in Utopia.
    true   false

Elizabeth was a queen.
    true   false

Elizabeth wanted her people to be rich.
    true   false

Read each main sentence below. Then read the statements that follow. Decide if each statement is true or false and circle your answer.

Michele had a birthday party on June 22. There were pony rides and games. Her favorite present was a pink dress.

Michele's birthday is in the winter.
    true   false

Michele had a pony at her party.
    true   false

Michele's favorite present was a pink blouse.
    true   false

Coco the pony loved giving rides to children. She worked at many birthday parties.

Coco was a racehorse.
    true   false

Coco was afraid of children.
    true   false

Coco went to many parties.
    true   false

Each sentence below is the answer to a question. On the line above each sentence, write the question.

_____

Lindsay is nine years old.

_____

Eddie is taking science, art, math, and reading.

_____

Randy made lasagna for dinner.

_____

The Blakes traveled to San Francisco for their vacation.

Each sentence below is the answer to a question. On the line above each sentence, write the question.

_____

Jennifer slept in a tent under a giant redwood tree.

_____

There will be a full moon tomorrow night.

_____

The statue is seven inches tall.

_____

Michael had juice, cereal, and toast for breakfast.

Draw a line from each question on the left side of the page to the correct answer on the right side of the page. Look for clues in each question that will help you find the right answer.

What kinds of animals live near their house?	They live in a house on Mud Bay.
Can we drive to Dan and Jeanne's house?	To visit them, their friends have to cross the bay at low tide.
Where do Dan and Jeanne live?	Around their house they see moose, porcupines, and eagles.
How do their friends get to see them?	No, no roads lead to Dan and Jeanne's house.
What kinds of trees grow around their house?	They live among spruce trees and alder trees.

Draw a line from each question on the left side of the page to the correct answer on the right side of the page. Look for clues in each question that will help you find the right answer.

Where do most of the salmon in the United States live?

They swim upstream to return to the place where they were born to lay eggs.

When do salmon spawn?

Most salmon live in Alaska.

How are salmon able to find the place where they were born?

A spawning ground is the place where salmon were born and where they lay their eggs.

What is a spawning ground?

Scientists have many theories, but no one knows for sure.

Why do salmon swim upstream?

Salmon swim upstream to reproduce in late summer.

Draw a line from each question on the left side of the page to the correct answer on the right side of the page. Look for clues in each question that will help you find the right answer.

Where are Ali and her family going for their vacation?

That was a glacier calving.

What is a glacier?

They are going to Glacier National Park.

What was that loud sound?

It is a river of ice created from an overload of snow in the mountains.

What is calving?

A chunk of ice that falls off the glacier and into water is called an iceberg.

What's a large piece of floating ice called?

Calving is when part of a glacier slides off onto the mountain below.

One rainy Saturday, Melissa and Eric went to a movie. They ate popcorn and candy and shared a large soda. The movie was about a family of grizzly bears.

Complete the sentences below so that they match the story.

Melissa and Eric saw a _____.

They shared a _____.

The movie was about _____.

Outside, the weather was _____.

For an extra challenge: On a separate piece of paper, write down some activities that Melissa and Eric could have done if it had not been raining.

Li Po and his father took a ferry ride along the west coast of Canada. They boarded the boat at night and immediately set up a tent on the deck. Each night, they slept in the tent on the deck of the ferry. During the day, they stood at the railing and looked at nature. They saw humpback whales and dolphins in the water, eagles in the sky, and deer on the islands that they traveled past.

Cross out the word in each sentence below that does not match the story. Replace it with another word or phrase that does match.

Li Po and his dad drove along the west coast of Canada.

_____

Seagulls flew over their heads. _____

Li Po and his dad slept in a cabin. _____

They boarded the ferry at noon. _____

Read the story, then answer the questions below.

Keith was walking through the desert when he came upon a scorpion in his path. The scorpion looked up at Keith and said, "May I sleep in your sleeping bag to keep warm?" Keith said, "No, you may not! However, you may sleep in one of my hiking boots. My feet have been warming them all day, so they should be very cozy." The scorpion thanked Keith. Then the scorpion reminded Keith to remove him in the morning before Keith put his boot back on.

Where did the scorpion want to sleep?

_____

Why didn't Keith agree to the scorpion's idea?

_____

Why do you think the scorpion asked Keith to remove him in the morning? _____
_____

Read the story, then answer the questions below.

Simon and Michelle were in the desert camping with their families. They decided to go for a walk to search for jackrabbits. After walking for a long time under the hot sun, they discovered a jackrabbit in their path. The jackrabbit, who had seen them first, stood before them and said, "Hello, Simon and Michelle. I have great news for you."

Where were Simon and Michelle camping? _____

What were Simon and Michelle looking for? _____

Do jackrabbits like hot weather or cold weather?

_____

What do you think the jackrabbit's news was?

_____

Read the story, then answer the questions below.

Travis the troll lived under a bridge. Travis was short and had a red beard. The people who lived in the town nearby all feared Travis. They had heard that Travis was scary and did not let people cross the bridge. But the truth was that Travis was a kind and gentle troll. He just did not know how to convince people that he meant them no harm.

Where did Travis live? _____

What did Travis look like? _____

Why did the people in the town fear Travis?

_____

Can you think of something that Travis could have done to change the way the people in the town thought of him?

_____

Read the story, then answer the questions below.

Andy works as a tour guide in Alaska. Every day, he goes down to the docks and picks up the tourists who have just arrived by boat. The tourists are always eager to see the animals of Alaska, such as the eagles, bears, and moose. Andy loves the tourists. He enjoys hearing about the cities and towns that they come from. Andy enjoys sharing his love of the land with the tourists.

What does Andy do for a living?

_____

What are the tourists eager to see?

_____

What does Andy like about his job?

_____

What would you like to see in Alaska?

_____

Read the story, then answer the questions below.

Bessie is a brown bear. She has two small cubs. Each day at dusk, she takes her cubs down to the river to fish for salmon. Bessie does most of the catching. One evening as the bears were fishing at the river, they saw a person. It was the first person the cubs had ever seen.

What is a cub?

_____

What do Bessie and her cubs do at the river?

_____

Why does Bessie do most of the catching?

_____

How do you think the cubs felt when they saw a person for the first time?

_____

Read each line of words. Think about what the words have in common. Then choose a word from the box below that continues the pattern. Write it on the line.

stove   sink   refrigerator   _____

streamers   balloons   party hats   _____

butter   ice   snow   _____

flat tire   strainer   Swiss cheese   _____

grass   frogs   paper money   _____

```
oven              confetti          candle
pickles           pineapple         donut
```

Read each pair of sentences. Fill in each blank line with a word that describes the words in **bold**.

Maria likes to eat lots of **apples, grapes, and bananas**.

Maria likes to eat lots of _____.

Kyle has a lot of **pennies, nickels, and dimes** in his piggy bank.

Kyle has lots of _____ in his piggy bank.

Audrey helped her mom set the table by putting out the **knives, forks, and spoons**.

Audrey helped her mom set the table by putting out the _____.

Dennis enjoys visiting the **monkeys, giraffes, and gorillas** at the zoo.

Dennis enjoys visiting the _____ at the zoo.

Read each pair of sentences. Fill in each blank line with a word that describes the words in **bold**.

Jen, Alexis, and Robert each put up their own tent.

The _____ each put up their own tent.

The children's mouths watered as they read about the **cake, ice cream, and pies** on the menu.

The children's mouths watered as they read about the _____ on the menu.

Becky raised many **cows, goats, and chickens** on her parents' farm.

Becky raised many _____ on her parents' farm.

Watching the **robins, pigeons, and blue jays** in the park tempted the cat.

Watching the _____ in the park tempted the cat.

Read each pair of sentences. Fill in each blank line with a word that describes the words in **bold**.

An entomologist studies **ants, bees, and flies**.

An entomologist studies

_____.

The **roses, irises, and gardenias** perfumed the air of Jo's garden.

The _____ perfumed the air of Jo's garden.

Every month, Marty liked to rearrange the **desk, chairs, and dresser** in his room.

Every month, Marty liked to rearrange the _____ in his room.

Amir played **soccer, hockey, and volleyball** in high school.

Amir played _____ in high school.

An **adjective** is a word that describes things. Circle the adjective in each sentence below. Then use the adjective in a new sentence.

Kevin told his family that he had seen an old man in the moon.

_____

Kevin's family said he was just a foolish boy.

_____

One dark night, Kevin took a picture of the man in the moon.

_____

He then had excellent proof that there was a man in the moon.

_____

Flick was a flea. He and his family lived on a long-haired golden retriever. Flick and his family loved roaming the golden forests of their dog. Sometimes their journeys would cause the dog to have an itch. When the dog scratched, it felt like an earthquake to Flick and his family. The dog's body shook, and they tumbled about as the dog's giant paw scratched the skin they lived on. One day, the skin shook so much that Flick was thrown off the dog.

Write an ending for the story using some of the adjectives in the box below.

_____

_____

_____

_____

_____

sad	fuzzy	excited
tall	hopeless	tired
loving	slick	frisky

Read the phrase below each picture. Decide whether the phrase tells who, what, when, where, why, or how. These words are called **question words** because we use them when we ask questions. Write the appropriate question word on the line below each phrase.

in the garden

_____

because she
was hungry

_____

ate all the lettuce

_____

during the night

_____

the bunny

_____

Put the phrases together to make a sentence. Write the sentence on the lines below.

_____

_____

Pronouns are words that sometimes take the place of nouns. Some pronoun words are **he, she, it, you,** and **they**.

Read each pair of sentences below. Decide what noun or nouns each pronoun in **bold** stands for. Write what the pronoun stands for in the space provided. Then make up an answer to the question following the sentences. Be sure to use at least one pronoun in your answer.

The caterpillars turned into butterflies.

Then **they** flew to the tops of the trees.

The pronoun **they** stands for _____.

What color were the butterflies? _____

Jeffrey wanted to be an actor when he grew up.

He liked to act in the school plays.

The pronoun **he** stands for _____.

Why do you think Jeffrey wanted to be an actor?

_____

During the summer, Hope takes many classes. She takes ballet every Wednesday. On Tuesdays, she takes a pottery class. Each Saturday, she joins her team in a track meet.

On what day might Hope make a flowerpot?

_____

What does Hope do on the day before Sunday?

_____

If today were Tuesday, what class would Hope be in tomorrow?

_____

On which days is Hope free?

_____

Read the story, then answer the questions below.

There once was a fairy named Galina. She lived under a large leaf in the tiny town of Apalonia with many other fairies. Galina loved to make children's wishes come true. Every day, Galina would fly out from under her leaf and into the world of people. She flew until she found a child who was making a wish. Then she would make the wish come true.

Where did Galina live?

_____

What did Galina love to do?

_____

Why do you think Galina loved to do this?

_____

What do you think the other fairies did every day?

_____

Read the paragraph below, then answer the questions. You will need to think about what the paragraph says and then draw your own conclusions.

Tinkerbell was a kitten. Her favorite toy was a ball of yarn. One day, her owner took the yarn to knit a sweater. After many days, Tinkerbell's owner finished the sweater. That night, Tinkerbell found the sweater lying on the couch.

Why do you think the ball of yarn was Tinkerbell's favorite toy?

_____

_____

How do you think Tinkerbell felt when her owner took the yarn?

_____

What do you think Tinkerbell did when she found the sweater?

_____

Do you think Tinkerbell will still like toys when she is older?

_____

Read the story, then answer the questions below.

Dave likes to hear tales about his great-great-grandfather in the gold rush days of California. The gold rush took place in the 1840s, over 150 years ago. During this time, men from all over the world traveled to California to dig for gold. All the men had dreams of finding gold and becoming rich. Dave's great-great-grandfather was one of the few lucky miners who struck it rich.

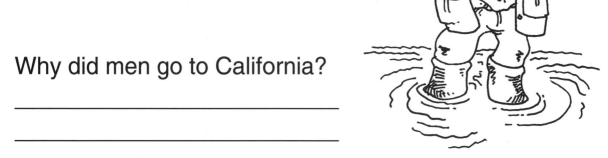

Why did men go to California?

_____

_____

Why do you think they called it the gold rush?

_____

What is a miner?

_____

Do you think Dave's great-great-grandfather is still alive today? Why or why not?

_____

Read the directions for how to make an ice-cream sundae. Then answer the questions below.

First, gather all the ingredients. You will need vanilla ice cream, chocolate syrup, whipped cream, nuts, and a cherry. Put a big scoop of ice cream in a tall sundae dish. Pour some chocolate syrup over the ice cream. Then put another scoop of ice cream on top of the first scoop. Pour more chocolate syrup over the ice cream. Cover the syrup with lots of whipped cream. Sprinkle nuts over the whipped cream. Last, place a cherry on top.

How many scoops of ice cream do you need?

_____

Do you put the nuts on the sundae before or after the whipped cream?

_____

What do you do last?

_____

What changes would you make to these directions?

_____

Sam is a very talented young painter. His mom always says, "Sam, your paintings are beautiful." Tomorrow, Sam's mom is having a birthday. Sam wants to give his mom a special present. He knows that she really likes yellow roses.

What do you think will happen next? Write an ending for the story.

_____

_____

_____

_____

_____

Ralph was teaching his friend Ivan how to throw a baseball. One day, they were practicing outside in front of their houses. Ivan threw the baseball really hard, but his aim was not very good. The ball went over Ralph's head and smashed a car window. Ivan and Ralph went to look at the damage. "Oh, no!" said Ivan. "This is Mr. Karloff's car!" Mr. Karloff was a very grumpy man who often yelled at the children for playing near the cars on the street.

What do you think happened next? Write an ending for the story.

_____

_____

_____

_____

_____

Answers

Page 5

music   soft
sticky   tool
Stories will vary.

Page 6

sport   cats
vegetables   tree
Stories will vary.

Page 7

Parent: Make sure child colors the picture as follows:
toy horse – brown
ball – purple
fire engine – red
kite – orange
skates – green

Pages 8–9

The teacher's desk has four drawers is a true statement.
Parent: Additions to the drawing should show child's comprehension of the text.

Page 10

Sample sentences:
The old woman used a cane to walk.
The gray kitten curled up on the blanket.
The tired teacher stayed up late marking tests.
The oak tree lost its leaves in the winter.
The little girl wore yellow sneakers.
The talented artist painted a colorful picture.
The great chef made a delicious meal.

Page 11

blue, humming, song – bird
cup, sponge, layer – cake
sweet, green, black-eyed – pea
Swiss, cheddar, jack – cheese
potato, corn, chocolate – chip

Page 12

Titles will vary.

Page 13

Titles will vary.

Page 14

Color this picture:

Page 15

Page 16

Circle this brochure:

Page 17

Change *happy* to *sad.*
Change *pumpkin* to *sandwich.*
Change *grows* to *paints.*
Change *nose* to *hand.*

Page 18

Change *sand* to *ketchup.*
Change *angry* to *happy.*
Change *teeth* to *cheeks.*
Change *lazy* to *careful.*
Extra challenge: Sentences will vary.

Page 19

Change *moon* to *sun.*
Change *broccoli* to *hay.*
Change *cookies* to *apples.*
Change *smelled* to *heard.*
Extra challenge: Sentences will vary.

Page 20

Change *freezer* to *dishwasher.*
Change *excited* to *frightened, scared,* or *afraid.*
Change *dryer* to *television.*
Change *ankle* to *finger.*
Change *pajamas* to *clothes.*
Change *quietly* to *fast.*

Page 21

Change *pie* to *hot dog* or *hamburger.*
Change *paint* to *cross.*
Change *dryer* to *oven.*
Change *statue* to *picture* or *photograph.*
Change *turtle* to *dog.*
Change *swim* to *comb* or *brush.*

Page 22

Pictures will vary.
Parent: Make sure child's picture illustrates a part of the story.

Answers

Page 23

__5__ Rinse off the dog's fur.
__4__ Work the shampoo into a lather.
__2__ Wet the dog's fur.
__1__ Catch the dog.
__3__ Pour some shampoo on the dog.
__6__ Dry the dog with a towel.
__X__ Make sure it is a sunny day.

Page 24

Jonathan can fly.
Samson has stripes.
A ponderosa has pine needles.
Extra challenge: Statements will vary.

Page 25

burros
hawks
name
snake
frightened
harmless

Page 26

Circle these books:
Neil Armstrong: First Man on the Moon
Elephants Never Forget
The Art of Cake Decorating

Page 27

Answers will vary, though words likely to be in the song are:
magic   wish
rub   granted
Rest of answers will vary.

Page 28

dry
after
trout

Summer
sunny
plant

Page 29

before   after

after   before

Page 30

cold
never
mend
day
proud

Page 31

false
false
true

true
false
true

Page 32

false
true
false

true
false
false

Page 33

false
true
false

false
false
true

Page 34

How old is Lindsay?
What classes is Eddie taking?
What did Randy make for dinner?
Where did the Blakes go for their vacation?

Page 35

Where did Jennifer sleep?
When will there be a full moon?
How tall is the statue?
What did Michael have for breakfast?

Page 36

What kinds of animals live near their house? — Around their house they see moose, porcupines, and eagles.
Can we drive to Dan and Jeanne's house? — No, no roads lead to Dan and Jeanne's house.
Where do Dan and Jeanne live? — They live in a house on Mud Bay.
How do their friends get to see them? — To visit them, their friends have to cross the bay at low tide.
What kinds of trees grow around their house? — They live among spruce trees and alder trees.

Page 37

Where do most of the salmon in the United States live? — Most salmon live in Alaska.
When do salmon spawn? — Salmon swim upstream to reproduce in late summer.
How are salmon able to find the place where they were born? — Scientists have many theories, but no one knows for sure.
What is a spawning ground? — A spawning ground is the place where salmon were born and where they lay their eggs.
Why do salmon swim upstream? — They swim upstream to return to the place where they were born to lay eggs.

Page 38

Where are Ali and her family going for their vacation? — They are going to Glacier National Park.
What is a glacier? — It is a river of ice created from an overload of snow in the mountains.
What was that loud sound? — That was a glacier calving.
What is calving? — Calving is when part of a glacier slides off onto the mountain below.
What's a large piece of floating ice called? — A chunk of ice that falls off the glacier and into water is called an iceberg.

Page 39

movie
large soda
a family of grizzly bears
rainy
Extra challenge: Answers will vary.

Page 40

Change *drove* to *took a ferry ride.*
Change *seagulls* to *eagles.*
Change *cabin* to *tent.*
Change *noon* to *night.*

Page 41

In Keith's sleeping bag.
Sample answer: Because he didn't want to share his sleeping bag with a scorpion.
Sample answer: So Keith wouldn't step on him.

Page 42

In the desert.
Jackrabbits.
Hot weather.
Answers will vary.

Page 43

Under a bridge.
Travis was short and had a red beard.
Because they had heard that Travis was scary and did not let people cross the bridge.
Answers will vary.

Page 44

Andy is a tour guide.
The animals of Alaska.
Andy enjoys hearing about the cities and towns that the tourists come from and enjoys sharing his love of the land with them.
Answers will vary.

Page 45

A young bear.
They fish for salmon.
Sample answer: Because she is older and has more experience catching salmon.
Answers will vary.

Page 46

oven (all are found in a kitchen)
confetti (all are party items)
candle (all melt)
donut (all have holes)
pickles (all are green)

Page 47

fruit
coins *or* money
utensils *or* cutlery
animals

Page 48

children
desserts
animals
birds

Page 49

insects
flowers
furniture
sports

Page 50

old
foolish
dark
excellent
Sentences will vary.

Page 51

Stories will vary.

Page 52

in the garden – where
because she was hungry – why
ate all the lettuce – what
during the night – when
the bunny – who
The bunny ate all the lettuce in the garden during the night because she was hungry.

Page 53

butterflies

Sample answer: They were yellow.
Jeffrey
Sample answer: Because he liked to dress in costumes and pretend to be other people.

Page 54

Tuesday
She joins her team in a track meet.
ballet
Sunday, Monday, Thursday, and Friday

Page 55

Under a large leaf in the tiny town of Apalonia.
She loved to make children's wishes come true.
Rest of answers will vary.

Page 56

Answers will vary.

Page 57

To find gold.
Because men rushed to California to find gold.
A person who digs in the ground to search for gold, silver, coal, or other materials.
No, Dave's great-great-grandfather could not be alive today because he lived over 150 years ago.

Page 58

two
after
Place a cherry on top.
Answers will vary.

Page 59

Answers will vary.

Page 60

Answers will vary.

Other

books that will help develop your child's gifts and talents

Workbooks:

- Reading (4–6) $4.95
- Reading Book Two (4–6) $4.95
- Math (4–6) $4.95
- Math Book Two (4–6) $4.95
- Language Arts (4–6) $4.95
- Puzzles & Games for
  Reading and Math (4–6) $4.95
- Puzzles & Games for
  Reading and Math Book Two (4–6) $4.95
- Puzzles & Games for
  Critical and Creative Thinking (4–6) $4.95
- Phonics (4–6) $4.95
- Phonics Puzzles & Games (4–6) $4.95
- Math Puzzles & Games (4–6) $4.95
- Reading Puzzles & Games (4–6) $4.95
- Reading (6–8) $4.95
- Reading Book Two (6–8) $4.95
- Math (6–8) $4.95
- Math Book Two (6–8) $4.95
- Language Arts (6–8) $4.95
- Puzzles & Games for
  Reading and Math (6–8) $4.95
- Puzzles & Games for
  Reading and Math Book Two (6–8) $4.95
- Puzzles & Games for
  Critical and Creative Thinking (6–8) $4.95
- Phonics (6–8) $4.95
- Phonics Puzzles & Games (6–8) $4.95
- Math Puzzles & Games (6–8) $4.95
- Reading Puzzles & Games (6–8) $4.95
- Reading Comprehension (6–8) $4.95
- Reading Comprehension Book Two (6–8) $4.95

Story Starters:

- My First Stories (6–8) $5.95
- Stories About Me (6–8) $5.95
- Stories About Animals (6–8) $4.95

Reference Workbooks:

- Word Book (4–6) $4.95
- Almanac (6–8) $3.95
- Animal Almanac (6–8) $6.95
- Atlas (6–8) $3.95
- Dictionary (6–8) $3.95

Science Workbooks:

- The Human Body (4–6) $5.95
- Animals (4–6) $5.95
- The Earth (4–6) $5.95
- The Ocean (4–6) $5.95
- Dinosaurs (6–8) $5.95

Question & Answer Books:

- The Gifted & Talented® Question &
  Answer Book for Ages 4–6 $5.95
- Gifted & Talented® More Questions &
  Answers for Ages 4–6 $5.95
- Gifted & Talented® Still More
  Questions & Answers for
  Ages 4–6 $5.95
- The Gifted & Talented® Question &
  Answer Book for Ages 6–8 $5.95
- Gifted & Talented® More Questions &
  Answers for Ages 6–8 $5.95
- Gifted & Talented® Still More
  Questions & Answers for
  Ages 6–8 $5.95
- Gifted & Talented® Science Questions
  & Answers: The Human Body
  for Ages 6–8 $5.95
- Gifted & Talented® Science Questions
  & Answers: Animals
  for Ages 6–8 $5.95

For Preschoolers:

- Alphabet Workbook $5.95
- Counting Workbook $5.95

For orders, call 1-800-323-4900.